IELTS

General Writing

Task 1

All you need to know to write a good letter

IELTSedits

IELTS

General Writing

Task 1

All you need to know to write a good letter

ISBN: 978-0-9933668-3-3

For further information e-mail the IELTSedits team at:

IELTSedits@gmail.com

Visit our website for FREE IELTS material - www.ieltsedits.com

The IELTSedits Team

The IELTSedits team — the authors of **Academic Word List in Use** and **Academic IELTS - Task 1 Writing** — are also able to help IELTS students wanting to further improve not only their vocabulary. but other IELTS exam skills.

Improve your IELTS Writing

As one of the more difficult IELTS skills to master, it takes time to develop the experience needed to get grade 7.0 and above in writing.

However, IELTSedits offers you the chance to help your writing skills improve more quickly and learn how to write IELTS tasks the way the examiner wants to see them.

We not only offer lots of writing tips but we can also suggest ways for you to improve by sending you a Student Report for every writing task you write.

For more information write to the IELTSedits team at - **IELTSedits@gmail.com**

Contents

Introduction

Nowadays, if people want to communicate in writing to someone else it is usually by email, SMS (text messages) or MSN. Text language has become the norm - LOL, BTW, IMHO are just a few of the many abbreviations commonly used.

It seems that the art of writing a letter is a thing of the past.

However, people who want to take the General IELTS exam need to be able to write a formal or informal letter that is at least 150 words in length and do this in about 20 minutes. This is Writing Task 1.

By following the suggestions given in this book, and with some actual writing practice, you will find that you will be able to write the kind of letter that will impress the examiner and, more importantly, get the grade you need.

A typical question is:

You should spend about 20 minutes on this task.

An English-speaking friend wants to spend a two-week holiday in your region and has written asking for information and advice.

Write a letter to your friend. In your letter,

- offer to find somewhere to stay
- give advice about what to do
- give information about what clothes to bring

Write at least 150 words.

You do **NOT** need to write any addresses.

Begin your letter as follows:

Dear Sir or Madam,

Types of Letter

As you start to see more examples of IELTS General Writing Task 1 letters, you will know that there are a range of different types of letters that you might be asked to write.

You need to become familiar with as many of them as possible if you want to have a good chance of getting a good grade.

Each letter has a main purpose or reason for writing the letter and these can be divided into a number of categories. The main reasons for writing a letter are:

- Thanking someone - e.g. a birthday present

- Complaining about someone or something - e.g. a bad meal at a restaurant

- Apologizing about something - e.g. a noisy party that you recently had

- Inviting someone to something - e.g. to a party

- Leaving something - a job, a club (e.g. a fitness club), your country to study

- Applying for something - e.g. a part-time job

- Recommending someone or something - e.g. a museum that you have been to

- Requesting information - e.g. about a short course at a local college

N.B.
There can be overlapping question types. For example, you might be thanking someone for a recent holiday but also inviting them to come and visit you. This is 'thanking someone' and 'inviting someone to something'. So, read the instructions carefully.

What is the Examiner Looking for?

It is possible to divide what the examiner is looking for when he reads your letter into four criteria.

Task Achievement

You need to provide information for all three bullet points and use the correct tone (formal or informal) throughout the letter.

Coherence and Cohesion

You need to use paragraphs, one for each bullet point, as well as write an appropriate opening and closing statement. You also need to link ideas together. Make sure that each bullet point remains in order, and separate from the other points, so that bullet point one becomes the first main body paragraph and so on.

Lexical resource

You need to use vocabulary that is appropriate for the topic. If the tone is formal then you cannot use informal vocabulary and vice versa.

Grammatical Range and Accuracy

You need to use a range of simple and complex sentence structures and avoid making too many errors.

If you can do all of this you are well on the way to getting a good grade.

Common Mistakes

Avoiding these common mistakes will help you improve your letter writing skills as well as increase your grade.

- ♦ Not long enough. You MUST reach the minimum word requirement of 150 words

- ♦ Change in tone - the beginning and ending of the letter don't match

- ♦ Wrong tone - You wrote the letter in the wrong 'tone' - formal or informal

- ♦ The letter doesn't 'flow' well because ideas are badly organized

- ♦ The main purpose of the letter isn't clear

- ♦ You didn't cover all three points

- ♦ You wrote too much about one point, and under developed the others

- ♦ Several points are put into one paragraph

- ♦ You didn't separate your paragraphs clearly

- ♦ Verb tenses are not always correct

- ♦ Vocabulary choice is not always accurate and may mix formal / informal styles

- ♦ The Task 1 instructions are copied

- ♦ Sentences are often too short showing a lack of grammatical control

Check List -

You can use this list of common mistakes as a check list when proofreading your answers.

Main Purpose of the Letter

The main purpose of the letter is stated in the first sentence of the information given to you in the Task 1 instructions. This gives you the direction as well as the tone of the letter.

If you see the word 'manager', 'boss', 'bank', and so on, then the letter is going to be formal.

If you see the word 'friend', 'classmate', 'flat mate', and so on, then the letter is going to be informal.

When you write your letter it is important not to copy long phrases from the information given to you. The examiner will not count these words and so this might mean that some students fail to reach the minimum of 150 words. **DO NOT COPY!**

It is OK, however, to use the key words, or most important words, and short phrases as these provide the focus for the letter and can help you to develop the bullet points that follow.

As you read the Task 1 instructions, it is a good idea, therefore, to underline words that you need to put into the letter. This will help remind you what are essential words and can not be missed out when you are writing the letter.

The Tone of a Letter

Setting the tone of a letter is an essential part of writing a good letter. There are varying levels of formality and informality but for the purposes of the letters you need to write in the IELTS exam we can simplify this and work with two basic styles - formal and informal.

Formal Letter

The formal letters will be when you are writing to someone you don't know or someone you don't know very well. This could be to a store to complain about a product that you bought - to a company to apply for a job - to a fitness club to tell them that you want to stop your membership, and so on.

Informal Letter

The informal letters will be when you are writing to someone that you know well and are on first name terms with. This could be to invite them to a house warming party - to ask them for information about a university that they attended - to thank them for a lovely weekend spent together, and so on.

Setting the Tone

The tone of the letter is set by:

- The way you begin the letter.

- The way you end the letter.

- Vocabulary

Vocabulary

While the way you begin and end the letter: sets the tone,

- Dear Mr. Smith, / Yours sincerely,

- Hi John, / See you soon,

You need to continue this tone in the three main paragraphs. You do this by the vocabulary and the phrases that you choose. While some words and phrases are more neutral and can be used in both formal and informal letters others are clearly one or the other.

Formal Letters

Never use contractions like - I'm, they've, and so on. You need to write the words in full - I am, they have, and so on.

Informal Letters

Contractions can and should be used as this shows the examiner that you know they can be used, and you know how to use them, in informal letters.

Examples of formal and informal phrases

Formal	Informal
my house	my place
I really enjoyed meeting you	It was great to see you
I really appreciate your help	Thanks for your help
I rarely have time to go now	I go there once in a blue moon
Last week I met my landlord	Today I bumped into Charles

How to Start

To start the letter you should get used to doing things in a certain way. If you always do certain things in a certain order it becomes very difficult to forget something. Forgetting things can result in a lower grade.

As you work through the different types of letters you will be given sentences for the opening and closing statements, and vocabulary and phrases that can be used for the bullet points.

You might need to use a dictionary for some of the vocabulary but this is how you will develop higher level vocabulary that is specific for Task 1 letters.

Here is a check list of things to do.

1. Salutations

2. Opening statement

3. Bullet point - 1

4. Bullet point - 2

5. Bullet point - 3

6. Closing statement

7. Closures

8. Your name

Beginning / Ending a Letter

Salutations and Closures

It's a good idea to study the beginnings and endings of your letter together because, if done correctly, these show the examiner that you have understood a very important part of writing a good letter. If done incorrectly then you have mixed formal and informal styles.

Salutations are how you begin a letter and address the person you are writing to. Examples are - Dear Sir or Madam, Dear Mr. White, Hi John,

Closures are what you say just before you write your name at the end of the letter and these must reflect the same tone as used in the salutations. Examples are - Yours sincerely, Best regards, See you soon,

Formal Letters

If you do not use the name of the person you are writing to you can use:

Dear Sir, / Yours faithfully,

Dear Madam, / Yours faithfully,

Dear Sir or Madam, / Yours faithfully,

OR

If you do know the name of the person you are writing to but use their family name rather than only their first name, or their first name and family name, you can use:

Dear Mr. Smith, / Yours sincerely,

Dear Mrs. Smith, / Yours sincerely,

Dear Ms. Mary Smith, / Yours sincerely,

N.B.
Don't forget to add the comma after - faithfully - and - sincerely.

Writing: Dear Sir or Madam, - Yours sincerely, is wrong.

Writing: Dear Mr. Smith, - Yours faithfully, is wrong.

Informal Letters

If you know the person well and write to them using their first name you can use:

Dear John, / See you soon,

Dear Mary, / Take care,

Dear Anne, / Best wishes,

Opening Statement

If the way you begin - the salutations - sets the tone of the letter the opening statement, in a formal letter, determines what the letter is about and sets the actual style of the letter. In an informal letter the opening statement can be a friendly greeting.

Look at the two extracts below complaining about a recent meal you had at a local restaurant:

Example 1

Dear Sir,

I am writing to complain about a meal my family and I recently had at your restaurant.

Example 2

Dear Sir,

I am writing to complain about the absolutely disgusting meal my family and I recently had at your horrible restaurant.

While both examples start the same way with a formal salutation, Example 2 has an aggressive style that might be deserved but is too angry for an IELTS type letter. Complain but be nice about it!

Formal Letters
You can say why you are writing in the first sentence - I am writing to apply for the job I saw advertised on your company website.

Informal Letters
You can use the first sentence to give some kind of greeting - It seems such a long time since we last met.

Opening Statement Phrases

Formal

- Thanking someone
    I am writing to thank you for the lovely time I had last night at your dinner party.

- Complaining about someone or something
    I am writing to express my dissatisfaction with the service my family received at your restaurant last weekend.

- Apologizing about something
    I am writing to apologize for the noise coming from my house last Friday.

- Inviting someone to something
    I am writing to invite you to my 21st birthday party this Saturday.

- Leaving something
    I am writing to inform you that I will be stopping my membership at your fitness club from the end of July.

- Applying for something
    I am writing in regard to the position of Chief Accountant which I saw advertised in the Daily Herald last Thursday.

- Recommending someone or something
    I am writing to inform you that the Regent Hotel on Warwick Street would be ideal for our annual staff dinner.

- Requesting information
    I am writing to request the exact starting date and tuition fee for your 3 week Computer 101 class.

Opening Statement Phrases

Informal

- Thanking someone
  Many thanks for the great night last night!

- Complaining about someone or something
  The food in your restaurant last night was not very good.

- Apologizing about something
  Sorry about all the noise the other night.

- Inviting someone to something
  Another year older! Please come to my party this Saturday.

- Leaving something
  I'm so busy at the moment that I will have to stop my membership for a while.

- Applying for something
  I am interested in the job you advertised in the paper.

- Recommending someone or something
  I want to pick the Regent Hotel for our annual staff dinner.

- Requesting information
  When does the 3 week Computer 101 class start and how much does it cost?

N.B.
Notice that the formal opening statements are usually longer than the informal ones and vocabulary is usually simpler for the latter.

Three Bullet Points

Each letter comes with three bullet points that MUST be answered in your letter.

For reasons of Cohesion and Coherence (one of the criteria used to judge your writing) it is a very good idea to use a separate paragraph for each bullet point and keep them in the same order that they are given to you.

So, three bullet points means three paragraphs. Each of these should be developed equally as much as possible with each paragraph being about 40 - 50 words.

To be able to develop each bullet point you have to do more than just answer the instructions.

For example:

Your neighbors have recently written to you to complain about the noise from your flat.

Write a letter to your neighbors. In your letter,

- explain the reasons for the noise
- apologize
- describe what action you will take

If you simply write:

I have started to learn the electric guitar.

I am very sorry about this.

I promise not to do this again.

You will certainly be under the required minimum of 150 words, even with the salutations and closures, and the examiner will be very unimpressed with your ability to develop ideas.

These bullet points must be developed by inventing, or making up, a story with realistic information that allows you to write more. Look at the example on the following page as to how this can be done.

Three Bullet Points

Your neighbors have recently written to you to complain about the noise from your flat.

Write a letter to your neighbors. In your letter,

- explain the reasons for the noise
- apologize
- describe what action you will take

Dear Neighbor,

I am writing to you in response to your letter complaining about the noise I have been making.

I recently started to learn the electric guitar because this is something I have always been interested in but never had the time to study. Now I have graduated from university I can devote some of my time to this.

I apologize for causing such a problem for you. I did not know that you work at the local hospital at night and need to sleep during the day. I can understand how frustrated and angry this must have made you.

Now that I know the situation I will only practice my guitar at night when you are working. If they are not too expensive, I will buy a set of headphones so I can use them when I am playing. I do not want to annoy any other neighbors.

I am very sorry for causing a problem for you and promise not to do this again.

Yours faithfully,

Eric Clapton

N.B.
This is now 171 words in total. You can see how the original ideas have been developed and turned into a realistic letter of apology for a situation that could really have happened.

Closing Statement Phrases

Formal Letters

The closing statement in a formal letter can act to stress the action you recommended in one of the main paragraphs. For example:

I hope that you treat this matter as urgent and rectify this mistake as quickly as possible.

I do hope that you are able to get back to me as soon as possible.

I look forward to hearing from you.

I look forward to your prompt response.

I expect to hear from you soon.

Thank you for your attention to this matter.

Please feel free to contact me for more information.

Please let me know if I can help in this matter.

Closing Statement Phrases

Informal Letters

The closing statement in an informal letter can act as a way to end with a friendly little message. For example:

I hope to see you soon.

See you next weekend.

I can't wait to hear from you.

I am looking forward to seeing you again.

Do let me know as soon as you can.

Thanks again for such a great time.

I can't wait to see you again.

Don't forget to tell Stella the news.

N.B.
When writing an informal letter you can often move from the closing statement straight to your name - missing out the closure - as they are often serving the same purpose. Or, add a closure and go straight to your name. However, it is good to use both in formal letters.

Thanking someone

Exercise

Last week you went to a restaurant in a local hotel to celebrate your birthday with some friends. It was a wonderful success and you all had a fantastic evening.

Write a letter to the restaurant. In your letter,

- mention the excellent food
- the service and atmosphere
- suggest improvements to make things better

You should spend about 20 minutes on this task.

Write at least 150 words.

You do **NOT** need to write any addresses.

Begin your letter as follows:

Dear Sir or Madam,

Writing Tips

Opening Statement - I am writing to you to thank you and your staff for a wonderful evening.

Closing Statement - Once again, many thanks for making our birthday celebration special.

Vocabulary
wonderful decor
extensive menu
attentive service
excellent value
relaxing atmosphere

Useful phrases
the bathroom needs renovating
the food was sublime
an evening to remember
a most memorable evening
I must congratulate you on providing a first class dinner

N.B.
Not all of the vocabulary and phrases presented here are used in the sample letter but it is recommended that you study them all and try to use them when possible.

Thanking someone

SAMPLE ESSAY

Dear Sir or Madam,

I am writing to you to thank you and your staff for the wonderful evening we had last Friday to celebrate my birthday.

We were all very impressed with the menu that you specially prepared for us and felt that the food was sublime. I was particularly impressed with the salmon and would have to say that it was the best I have ever eaten. The desserts were just out of this world and enjoyed by everybody.

The waiters deserve a special mention as they were so attentive and made the selection of each dish much easier than it could have been. Nothing seemed too much trouble for them. They are all good ambassadors for your hotel's restaurant, and added greatly to the atmosphere that evening.

While I will certainly recommend you to anyone that will listen, I must tell you that a number of people in our party were rather shocked by the condition of the bathrooms. Toilets would not flush properly, faucets were leaking and there were no paper towels to dry our hands. Please renovate them and upgrade the facilities.

Once again, many thanks for making our birthday celebration special.

Yours faithfully,

John McEnroe

Thanking someone

Exercise

Last month you had a memorable holiday with some friends where you stayed at their house. They have just sent you some holiday photos.

Write a letter to your friends. In your letter,

- thank them for the holiday and the photos
- explain why you didn't write earlier
- invite them to come and stay with you

You should spend about 20 minutes on this task.

Write at least 150 words.

You do **NOT** need to write any addresses.

Begin your letter as follows:

Dear _____ ,

Writing Tips

Opening Statement - A big hello to you all.

Closing Statement - I can't wait to see you guys again.

Vocabulary
great memories
fabulous photos
crazy deadline
backlog

Useful phrases
you really are a great photographer
you're so lucky to have such a beautiful house
I will frame the one of us at the swimming pool
up to my neck in work
it helped me recharge my batteries

N.B.
Not all of the vocabulary and phrases presented here are used in the sample letter but it is recommended that you study them all and try to use them when possible.

Thanking someone

Exercise

Last month you had a memorable holiday with some friends where you stayed at their house. They have just sent you some holiday photos.

Write a letter to your friends. In your letter,

- thank them for the holiday and the photos
- explain why you didn't write earlier
- invite them to come and stay with you

Thanking someone

Thanking someone

Complaining about someone or something

Exercise

You are a student at an English language school in Brighton and are living in private accommodation with other flat mates. You have not had hot water or heating for some time. The landlord's workmen have tried to fix the problem but without success.

Write a letter to the landlord. In your letter,

- state your reason for writing
- describe the problems and explain how you feel
- propose a solution and ask the landlord to take action

You should spend about 20 minutes on this task.

Write at least 150 words.

You do **NOT** need to write any addresses.

Begin your letter as follows:

Dear _____ ,

Writing Tips

Opening Statement - I am writing to complain about the heating system in the flat we are renting from you.

Closing Statement - I hope you are able to settle this issue as quickly as possible.

Vocabulary
heating system
frustrating
inconvenient
miserable
chores

Useful phrases
incapable of fixing it
very incompetent repairmen
once in a blue moon

N.B.
Not all of the vocabulary and phrases presented here are used in the sample letter but it is recommended that you study them all and try to use them when possible.

Complaining about someone or something

SAMPLE ESSAY

Dear Mr. Osbourne,

I am writing to complain about the heating system in the flat we are renting from you.

I have been living in your flat on Fleet Street for over 3 months now and have never had a reliable heating system. If we are very lucky it might turn on once in a blue moon but basically we can never rely on it and as a result have become greatly inconvenienced.

This has created so many problems for us because we all need to wash twice a day as well as wash the dishes and clothes. All of this has to be done using cold water which makes our chores almost unbearable as day by day it is getting colder. As the flat is never warm we always feel miserable and find it difficult to study.

As your workmen seem incapable of fixing it, they tried a few months ago, I suggest that we find someone to repair the heating system and then bill you accordingly. If you accept this idea then we will call someone that we have been recommended.

Please let me know if this suggestion is acceptable.

Best regards,

Tracy Chapman

N.B.
Best regards - would also work when writing an informal letter to a friend where you are only using the first name of the person. This person would probably not be your very best or closest friend but you know them too well to start the letter with, for example, Dear Mr. Greg Lake. You would also end with only your first name.

Complaining about someone or something

Exercise

You travelled by plane last week and your suitcase was lost. You have still heard nothing from the airline company.

Write to the airline. In your letter,

- explain what happened
- describe your suitcase and tell them what was in it
- find out what they are going to do about it

You should spend about 20 minutes on this task.

Write at least 150 words.

You do **NOT** need to write any addresses.

Begin your letter as follows:

Dear Sir or Madam,

Writing Tips

Opening Statement - I am writing to you to report a missing suitcase.

Closing Statement - I hope to hear good news from you as soon as possible.

Vocabulary
baggage carousel
Samsonite - Optic Spinner
metallic black
distinguishing feature
flight details

Useful phrases
I am now extremely worried
it cost me a little over
all other passengers had collected their bags
I sincerely hope that you will be able to help

N.B.
Not all of the vocabulary and phrases presented here are used in the sample letter but it is recommended that you study them all and try to use them when possible.

Complaining about someone or something

Exercise

You travelled by plane last week and your suitcase was lost. You have still heard nothing from the airline company.

Write to the airline. In your letter,

- explain what happened
- describe your suitcase and tell them what was in it
- find out what they are going to do about it

_____

_____

_____

_____

_____

_____

_____

_____

_____

_____

_____

_____

_____

_____

_____

_____

_____

_____

_____

Complaining about someone or something

_____

_____

_____

_____

_____

_____

_____

_____

_____

_____

_____

_____

_____

_____

_____

_____

_____

_____

_____

Complaining about someone or something

Apologizing about something

Exercise

You borrowed an important textbook from a classmate last term. You now realise your classmate has returned home overseas and you still have the book.

Write a letter to him/her. In your letter,

- apologise for the mistake
- find out how important the book is to him/her
- say what you will do

You should spend about 20 minutes on this task.

Write at least 150 words.

You do **NOT** need to write any addresses.

Begin your letter as follows:

Dear _____ ,

Writing Tips

Opening Statement - I hope you are enjoying your time at home with your family.

Closing Statement - Take care and enjoy the break.

Vocabulary
expensive textbook
international express mail service
semester
summer vacation

Useful phrases
It completely slipped my mind
I feel so incredibly embarrassed
I can assure you that I will send it to you
It was so generous of you to have lent it to me
I hope you are not so angry

N.B.
Not all of the vocabulary and phrases presented here are used in the sample letter but it is recommended that you study them all and try to use them when possible.

Apologizing about something

SAMPLE ESSAY

Dear Mary,

I hope you are enjoying your time at home with your family.

I am so sorry for not giving you back your book before you left for China. It helped me so much when studying that I really don't think I would have passed the exams without it. I left your book on my coffee table so I wouldn't forget to return it but it completely slipped my mind.

Please don't worry. The book is safe and still looks like new. How quickly do you need the book back? I am sure that it is very important to you and is a book you want to keep. Let me know if you want to review it during our summer vacation or if you are happy to wait until the start of next semester.

If you decide that you want it back ASAP then I am happy to pay DHL to send it to your home in China. Maybe you would prefer to have it before the next semester starts. Just send me your address and I will arrange this after the weekend and you should get it within 3 to 4 days.

Take care and enjoy the break.

Enya

Apologizing about something

Exercise

You have just spent a weekend at a friend's house. When you returned home, you discovered you have left a coat containing some belongings in his house.

Write a letter to your friend telling him that you left the coat. In your letter,

- tell him what the coat looks like
- where you think you left it and what was inside it
- make some suggestions about how to get it back and apologize for the inconvenience

You should spend about 20 minutes on this task.

Write at least 150 words.

You do **NOT** need to write any addresses.

Begin your letter as follows:

Dear _____ ,

Writing Tips

Opening Statement - You won't believe this, but I left my coat at your house last weekend.

Closing Statement - Thanks for your help.

Vocabulary
coat rack
bus pass
personal belongings
really inconvenient

Useful phrases
look behind the sofa
it's really freezing down here!
I wasn't thinking properly
before it gets too cold
I can't live without it

N.B.
Not all of the vocabulary and phrases presented here are used in the sample letter but it is recommended that you study them all and try to use them when possible.

Apologizing about something

Exercise

You have just spent a weekend at a friend's house. When you returned home, you discovered you have left a coat containing some belongings in his house.

Write a letter to your friend telling him that you left the coat. In your letter,

- tell him what the coat looks like
- where you think you left it and what was inside it
- make some suggestions about how to get it back

_____

_____

_____

_____

_____

_____

_____

_____

_____

_____

_____

_____

_____

_____

_____

_____

_____

_____

Apologizing about something

Apologizing about something

Inviting someone to something

Exercise

You have recently been to stay with an old friend for a few days. You hadn't seen each other for a long time.

Write a letter to him/her. In your letter,

- say how you felt about the visit
- refer to something enjoyable that you did while staying with him/her
- invite your friend to visit you

You should spend about 20 minutes on this task.

Write at least 150 words.

You do **NOT** need to write any addresses.

Begin your letter as follows:

Dear _____ ,

Writing Tips

Opening Statement - How lovely it was to see you again. You haven't changed a bit!

Closing Statement - Thank you once again for a really lovely time.

Vocabulary
spare bedroom
French bistro
special memories
spectacular scenery

Useful phrases
it was great to take a trip down memory lane
it was great to catch up on all your news
it's an open invitation to visit
what a great laugh it was to spend time with you again

N.B.
Not all of the vocabulary and phrases presented here are used in the sample letter but it is recommended that you study them all and try to use them when possible.

Inviting someone to something

SAMPLE ESSAY

Dear Jane,

How lovely it was to see you again. You haven't changed a bit!

I had such a wonderful time catching up on all your news. I can't believe it's been 7 years since we last met. The time I spent with you and your friends went in a blur of so many special memories. Thank you!

My favourite memory of this holiday was when we went to the French bistro near your apartment. The food there was fantastic and made even better by the live band. It really took me back to our student years when we shared a place together.

I really don't want to wait so long before meeting you again so why not come to my place for a holiday in the summer? I think I told you that I have a spare bedroom so there is no problem staying with me and we can visit all of the art galleries that we talked about this time.

Thank you once again for a really lovely time.

Lots of love,

Mary

Inviting someone to something

Exercise
You have recently moved to a different house.

Write a letter to an English-speaking friend. In your letter,

- explain why you have moved
- describe the new house
- invite your friend to come and visit

You should spend about 20 minutes on this task.

Write at least 150 words.

You do **NOT** need to write any addresses.

Begin your letter as follows:

Dear _____ ,

Writing Tips

Opening Statement - I hope you are well.

Closing Statement - Lots of love,

Vocabulary
spacious kitchen
open fire
breathtaking views
all mod cons

Useful phrases
I felt so cramped
help me celebrate
I would love you to come
a few friends that live nearby
closer to work

N.B.
Not all of the vocabulary and phrases presented here are used in the sample letter but it is recommended that you study them all and try to use them when possible.

Inviting someone to something

Exercise

You have recently moved to a different house.

Write a letter to an English-speaking friend. In your letter,

- explain why you have moved
- describe the new house
- invite your friend to come and visit

_____

_____

_____

_____

_____

_____

_____

_____

_____

_____

_____

_____

_____

_____

_____

_____

Inviting someone to something

Inventing someone to something

Leaving something

Exercise

For the past year you have been a member of a local club. Now you want to discontinue your membership.

Write a letter to the club secretary. In your letter,

- state what type of membership you have and how you have paid for this
- give details of how you have benefited from the club
- explain why you want to leave

You should spend about 20 minutes on this task.

Write at least 150 words.

You do **NOT** need to write any addresses.

Begin your letter as follows:

Dear Sir or Madam,

Writing Tips

Opening Statement - I am writing to you in connection with my membership at Gold's Gym in Miranda, New South Wales.

Closing Statement - Many thanks for having such wonderful facilities.

Vocabulary
personal assistant
equipment
facilities
low fitness levels

Useful phrases
more strength and a lot more energy
such knowledgeable staff
good value for money
easily the best gym in the area

N.B.
Not all of the vocabulary and phrases presented here are used in the sample letter but it is recommended that you study them all and try to use them when possible.

Leaving something

SAMPLE ESSAY

Dear Sir or Madam,

I am writing to you in connection with my membership at Gold's Gym in Miranda, New South Wales.

For the last 3 years I have held a full-time Fitness Plus membership card. Payments were always made every 3 months by using my Visa card. From time to time I would pay for special courses like the 'Tai Chi for Beginners' last summer.

When I first started at your gym I was starting with very low fitness levels after 6 months off work following a car accident. With wonderful help from your personal assistant – Geoff – I slowly began to gain more strength and a lot more energy.

I have been accepted at Deakin University in Victoria to study for my BA in molecular biology. This means that I am going to be pretty busy until I graduate. However, once I graduate, I promise that I will be back again at your gym.

Many thanks for having such wonderful facilities.

Yours faithfully,

Brian Eno

Leaving something

Exercise
A friend has agreed to look after your house and pet while you are on holiday.

Write a letter to your friend. In your letter,

- give contact details for when you are away
- give instructions about how to care for your pet
- describe other household duties

You should spend about 20 minutes on this task.

Write at least 150 words.

You do **NOT** need to write any addresses.

Begin your letter as follows:

Dear _____ ,

Writing Tips

Opening Statement - Just a few more things to tell you before I head off to the airport.

Closing Statement - Thanks again and see you when I get back.

Vocabulary
kitchen counter
kitchen cabinet
letter box
flower pot
tin of biscuits

Useful phrases
before I head off to the airport
if you feel peckish
the far left of the cooker
I'm so grateful you offered to help

N.B.
Not all of the vocabulary and phrases presented here are used in the sample letter but it is recommended that you study them all and try to use them when possible.

Leaving something

Exercise

A friend has agreed to look after your house and pet while you are on holiday.

Write a letter to your friend. In your letter,

- give contact details for when you are away
- give instructions about how to care for your pet
- describe other household duties

_____

_____

_____

_____

_____

_____

_____

_____

_____

_____

_____

_____

_____

_____

_____

_____

_____

_____

_____

Leaving something

_____

_____

_____

_____

_____

_____

_____

_____

_____

_____

_____

_____

_____

_____

_____

_____

_____

_____

_____

_____

_____

Leaving something

Applying for something

Exercise

You have seen an advertisement for part-time work in a hotel for three months over the summer.

Write a letter to the Manager. In your letter,

- say what experience you have
- ask what the work involves
- enquire about conditions

You should spend about 20 minutes on this task.

Write at least 150 words.

You do **NOT** need to write any addresses.

Begin your letter as follows:

Dear _____ ,

Writing Tips

Opening Statement - I am writing to you to apply for a part-time job in your hotel over the summer.

Closing Statement - I look forward to hearing from you.

Vocabulary
job description
monthly salary
prestigious hotel

Useful phrases
based on my experience
my expected salary
a golden opportunity to develop my skills
not afraid of hard work and long hours
I see my future in the hotel business

N.B.
Not all of the vocabulary and phrases presented here are used in the sample letter but it is recommended that you study them all and try to use them when possible.

Applying for something

SAMPLE ESSAY

Dear Mr. Edwards,

I am writing to you to apply for a part-time job in your hotel over the summer.

I do have some experience of working as a front office assistant two years ago at the Howard Plaza Hotel in London. I worked there for about 6 months from around the start of July and into the New Year. I had wonderful colleagues and I learnt a lot from them.

Because it was a very busy hotel, and at times under staffed, I was asked to do a lot of different things which I enjoyed. I had the chance to deal directly with guests as they arrived and checked out, I also had to cover for room service when they were too busy, and I also helped guests with their bags.

I would like to take this chance to ask you a few questions about the job itself. What would be the expected working hours per day and which day or days would be free? Based on my experience what would be my expected monthly salary? And one last thing - would you supply my uniform?

I look forward to hearing from you.

Yours sincerely,

Keith Richards

Applying for something

Exercise
You work in a busy but poorly organised office and you are keen to be promoted. Your employer needs to find a new supervisor for your department.

Write a letter to your employer. In the letter,

- ask to be considered for this job
- explain why you would be a suitable candidate
- outline the current problems and the changes you would like to make

You should spend about 20 minutes on this task.

Write at least 150 words.

You do **NOT** need to write any addresses.

Begin your letter as follows:

Dear Mr. _____ ,

Writing Tips

Opening Statement - I am writing to you in connection with the job advertised in this week's company newsletter.

Closing Statement - I hope to hear a favourable reply from you.

Vocabulary
quick turnover
official application form
company newsletter
training program
range of food products
maintaining quality

Useful phrases
I would like to be considered for the position of
one problem we have faced in recent years
I would like to take on this challenge
I understand that several interviews would be held

N.B.
Not all of the vocabulary and phrases presented here are used in the sample letter but it is recommended that you study them all and try to use them when possible.

Applying for something

Exercise

You work in a busy but poorly organised office and you are keen to be promoted. Your employer needs to find a new supervisor for your department.

Write a letter to your employer. In the letter,

- ask to be considered for this job
- explain why you would be a suitable candidate
- outline the current problems and the changes you would like to make

_____

_____

_____

_____

_____

_____

_____

_____

_____

_____

_____

_____

_____

_____

_____

_____

_____

_____

Applying for something

_____

_____

_____

_____

_____

_____

_____

_____

_____

_____

_____

_____

_____

_____

_____

_____

_____

_____

_____

_____

_____

_____

_____

Applying for something

Recommending someone or something

Exercise

Write a letter to your friend about a museum that you have visited. Write three paragraphs that focus on,

- where you went
- what you saw there
- how you felt about it

You should spend about 20 minutes on this task.

Write at least 150 words.

You do **NOT** need to write any addresses.

Begin your letter as follows:

Dear _____ ,

Writing Tips

Opening Statement - You'll never guess where I went last weekend!

Closing Statement - Bye for now,

Vocabulary
fabulous view
college friends
free time
incredible experience

Useful phrases
called me out of the blue
part of the exhibition
the best exhibition I have ever seen
have a bite to eat
it really is worth a visit
free to get in
well worth your time

N.B.
Not all of the vocabulary and phrases presented here are used in the sample letter but it is recommended that you study them all and try to use them when possible.

Recommending someone or something

SAMPLE ESSAY

Hi Bill,

You'll never guess where I went last weekend!

One of my college friends called me out of the blue last Saturday and invited me to the Generation X exhibition at the Tate Modern in Bankside. It doesn't open until 10 in the morning but it stays open until 10pm.

My favourite part of the exhibition was where they feature a lot of the Generation X rock stars like Billy Idol, Nirvana, and the Beastie Boys. They even have a fantastic place to sit and have a bite to eat and relax and look at the fabulous view over London.

I can honestly say that it was the best exhibition I have ever seen and you know I have been to many over the years. I could really have spent a lot more time there and might go again next week. If you have any free time it really is worth a visit.

Bye for now,

Paul

Recommending someone or something

Exercise

You eat at your college cafeteria every lunchtime. However, you think it needs some improvements.

Write a letter to the college magazine. In you letter,

- explain what you like about the cafeteria
- say what is wrong with it
- suggest how it could be improved

You should spend about 20 minutes on this task.

Write at least 150 words.

You do **NOT** need to write any addresses.

Begin your letter as follows:

Dear Sir or Madam,

Writing Tips

Opening Statement - I am writing to offer some insights in to my dining experience at our college cafeteria.

Closing Statement - I would be interested to hear other diner's comments.

Vocabulary
dining experience
streamlined
preparation area
dining experience

Useful phrases
to offer some insights
it is always piping hot
I hesitate to offer a solution
The prices are also very fair

N.B.
Not all of the vocabulary and phrases presented here are used in the sample letter but it is recommended that you study them all and try to use them when possible.

Recommending someone or something

Exercise

You eat at your college cafeteria every lunchtime. However, you think it needs some improvements.

Write a letter to the college magazine. In you letter,

- explain what you like about the cafeteria
- say what is wrong with it
- suggest how it could be improved

_____

_____

_____

_____

_____

_____

_____

_____

_____

_____

_____

_____

_____

_____

_____

Recommending someone or something

Recommending someone or something

Requesting information

Exercise

You have a friend who lives in a city abroad. You have decided that you would like to apply to do a course at one of the colleges in this city.

Write to your friend explaining,

- what you would like to do
- what type of work or studies you have been doing for the past few years
- ask for assistance in contacting an appropriate institution

You should spend about 20 minutes on this task.

Write at least 150 words.

You do **NOT** need to write any addresses.

Begin your letter as follows:

Dear _____ ,

Writing Tips

Opening Statement - I hope everything is going well.

Closing Statement - Many thanks,

Vocabulary
contact name and address
a long term future
my ambition

Useful phrases
I have finally decided
quit my job
little chance of promotion
while I am still young
in a rut

N.B.
Not all of the vocabulary and phrases presented here are used in the sample letter but it is recommended that you study them all and try to use them when possible.

Requesting information

SAMPLE ESSAY

Dear Charles,

I hope everything is going well.

I have finally decided that I am going to quit my job and take a Master's Degree in Paris. I want to take an MSc in electrical engineering as this is really the field I love and can see a long term future for me. Also, I would love to spend time in the City of Love!

As you know, I have been at AEG for 6 years and have learnt a lot about electrical engineering but I now seem to be in a bit of a rut. Everyone loves it here so there seems little chance of promotion and I really need to develop my career while I am still young.

As you have lived in Paris for a few years now I am hoping that you might be able to help find some colleges that teach electrical engineering and have a good reputation. I will write to them but if it is possible for you to find contact names and addresses I would really appreciate it.

Many thanks,

Billy

Requesting information

Exercise

You have just rented an unfurnished flat and a friend has told you that the Opportunity Shop in the shopping centre has cheap second-hand furniture.

Write to the shop owner asking him,

- what you need
- whether they have these items
- what they cost

You should spend about 20 minutes on this task.

Write at least 150 words.

You do **NOT** need to write any addresses.

Begin your letter as follows:

Dear Sir or Madam,

Writing Tips

Opening Statement - I am writing to enquire about some furniture I need.

Closing Statement - I look forward to hearing from you.

Vocabulary
an unfurnished flat
a small dining room table with chairs
on hire purchase
in stock

Useful phrases
just graduated from college
different pieces of furniture
maybe you can recommend something

N.B.
Not all of the vocabulary and phrases presented here are used in the sample letter but it is recommended that you study them all and try to use them when possible.

Requesting information

Exercise

You have just rented an unfurnished flat and a friend has told you that the Opportunity Shop in the shopping centre has cheap second-hand furniture.

Write to the shop owner asking him,

- what you need
- whether they have these items
- what they cost

_____

_____

_____

_____

_____

_____

_____

_____

_____

_____

_____

_____

_____

_____

_____

_____

_____

Requesting information

Requesting information

Answers

Thanking Someone

Dear Jim, Carol and kids,

A big hello to you all.

What a big surprise it was to see a big envelope waiting for me when I collected my mail a couple of weeks ago. What fabulous photos! You really are a great photographer Carol. They all brought back such great memories. I am going to frame the one of us at the swimming pool and put it above my desk in my office.

I am so sorry for not writing straight away. I've been up to my neck in work ever since I got back with a pile of work waiting for me on my first day back to work. I need another holiday to recharge my batteries again! Today is a national holiday so I've taken the chance to write and thank you for such a fantastic holiday and these lovely photos.

I couldn't believe that it was over 3 years since we last met. Time has certainly gone quickly since we all graduated. Now I have settled back into my routine again and caught up with the backlog, I would like to invite you to come and stay with me. I can take time off in the summer so just let me know when you can come and I will book time off.

I can't wait to see you guys again.

Carlos

Complaining about someone or something

Dear Sir or Madam,

I am writing to you to report a missing suitcase.

I was flying back to Sydney on Monday, August 15th on flight CX221 after a business trip to Singapore. After arriving in Sydney I went straight to the carousel to collect my bag. After waiting for over an hour and after all other passengers had collected their bags, I realised mine was lost.

My suitcase is a metallic black Samsonite Optic Spinner. It is the largest in that range and almost 80cm in height. It cost me a little over US$ 200 when I bought it last year in Australia. A distinguishing feature is a colored Mickey Mouse sticker on the front of the suitcase.

I did speak to a woman at the Cathay Pacific information desk and they recorded my bag as missing along with the flight details I have given to you above. Coming from a business trip some very important documents are in the bag which I need.

I hope to hear good news from you as soon as possible.

Yours faithfully,

Kate Perry

Apologizing about something

Dear Mick,

You won't believe this, but I left my coat at your house last weekend.

You can tell I had a good time at your place because I wasn't thinking properly by the time I left! If you remember it is the black trench coat with the big lapels and the brass buttons.

I am pretty certain that I must have left it on the coat rack in the kitchen but if it is not there then look behind the sofa as it might be there. It might have fallen behind it. Pick it up carefully because it has my bus pass in one of its pockets.

I hope that we can think of a way to get the coat back to me before it gets too cold here or else I will have to buy a new one. I'm really sorry to ask but could you come and visit me this weekend and bring it then?

Thanks for a great weekend.

Tony

Inviting someone to something

Dear Sue,

I hope you are well.

I am so excited to tell you that I have finally moved to a new house. After 3 years of living in the same place I finally had to move somewhere quieter and with more room. I felt so cramped in the old house and didn't even unpack some of my suitcases.

The new house is perfect. It's only about 3 years old so is very modern with a wonderful spacious kitchen and a bathroom with separate bath and shower. There are two bedrooms which is ideal. There is even a little garden at the front and back with enough space to have a BBQ in the summer.

I would love you to come and visit and help me celebrate my new house with a few friends that live nearby. I need a little time to unpack and really make the place seem like home. So, why don't we say June 23 -24? If that's OK, I will start to prepare things for when you arrive.

Lots of love,

Niki

Leaving something

Dear Steve,

Just a few more things to tell you before I head off to the airport.

You probably won't have to, but if you really need to, you can either write to my e-mail address – carlforeman@gmail.com – or if you need to contact me straight away you can call me on 98-1878- 235-745.

Here are the instructions for Misty. All her food is in the kitchen cabinet on the far left of the cooker. Give her one small can each meal. Two meals a day. For something to drink just make sure the bowl is half full of milk when you give her food. There is enough milk in the fridge to last until I get back.

The only other thing I can think of is to always pull any letters out of the letter box. Feel free to make yourself a cup of tea or coffee anytime you are in my house. You can use Misty's milk! There is a large tin of biscuits on the kitchen counter if you feel peckish!

Thanks again and see you when I get back.

Carl

P.S. The key is under the big flower pot by the front door.

Applying for something

Dear Mr. Jack Bruce,

I am writing to you in connection with the job advertised in this week's company newsletter.

I would like to be considered for the position of supervisor in the Quality Control Department and would, therefore, like to request an official application form from you. I understand that several interviews would be held if I am considered for this job.

As you know, I have worked in this department for over 6 years now and over that time have become familiar with all of the various aspects of maintaining the quality of our range of food products. I also helped to install most of the new equipment so am familiar with all of the new machines.

One problem we have faced in recent years is the quick turnover of staff in this department but I feel that this could be helped by providing a more complete training program for new employees. I would like to take on this challenge and develop a better program for our department.

I hope to hear a favourable reply from you as soon as possible.

Best regards,

Brian May

Recommending someone or something

Dear Sir or Madam,

I am writing to offer some insights in to my dining experience at our college cafeteria.

I have been using the college cafeteria every lunch time since I started my accountancy course 6 months ago. I love the variety of food which always seems fresh and it is always piping hot. The prices are also very fair.

I would like to take this opportunity, however, to mention one thing that does affect the dining experience there. There are always long queues in the cafeteria and so it takes up almost all of our lunch time to eat a simple meal.

I hesitate to offer a solution to this as I am only a student and have had no catering experience. Nevertheless, it seems as if the people in the serving area get in the way of those in the preparation area. I think if the cafeteria were to separate the two areas the whole process would be streamlined.

I would be interested to hear other diners' comments.

Yours faithfully,

Joey Ramone

Requesting information

Dear Sir or Madam,

I am writing to enquire about some furniture I need.

I recently moved to an unfurnished flat so I am looking for a number of different pieces of furniture. I will have to buy everything over time and so, for now, the main things I need are a single bed, a 3-seater sofa, a small dining room table with chairs, and a coffee table.

I am hoping that you might have some of these items in stock but if not then let me know if it is possible for you to get them. If you do not have exactly what I am looking for maybe you can recommend something close to it.

Also, I'm keen to know what sort of prices we are looking at for each of the items I have listed. I have only just graduated from college and am about to start my first job next month so money is limited. Is it possible to buy everything on hire purchase?

I look forward to hearing from you.

Yours faithfully,

Richard Branson

IELTSedits

Also written by the IELTSedits team -

Academic Word List in Use

Academic IELTS - Task 1 Writing

www.ingramcontent.com/pod-product-compliance
Lightning Source LLC
LaVergne TN
LVHW061227060426
835509LV00012B/1463